L-1.9/P-05

Compass Point

Phonics Readers

Now and Long Ago

by Wiley Blevins

Reading Consultant: Wiley Blevins, M.A.
Phonics/Early Reading Specialist

 COMPASS POINT BOOKS

Minneapolis, Minnesota

Compass Point Books
3109 West 50th Street, #115
Minneapolis, MN 55410

Visit Compass Point Books on the Internet at www.compasspointbooks.com
or e-mail your request to custserv@compasspointbooks.com

Photographs ©: Cover and p. 1 right: Corbis/Underwood & Underwood, Cover and p. 1 left:
Brand X Pictures/SWP, Inc., p. 6: PhotoDisc/Scott T. Baxter, p. 7: Corbis/Edouard Evartt
Exline, p. 8: Getty Images/Hulton/Archive, p. 9: DigitalVision, p. 10: Corbis/Hulton Deutsch
Collection, p. 11: Index Stock Imagery/Chris Minerva, p. 12: Corbis/Dave G. Houser

Editorial Development: Alice Dickstein, Alice Boynton
Photo Researcher: Wanda Winch
Design/Page Production: Silver Editions, Inc.

Library of Congress Cataloging-in-Publication Data
Blevins, Wiley.
  Now and long ago / by Wiley Blevins.
      p. cm. — (Compass Point phonics readers)
  Summary: Briefly introduces ways in which life was different in the
  past, such as farmers using hand-held plows instead of tractors, in a
  text that incorporates phonics instruction.
   ISBN 0-7565-0515-1 (hardcover : alk. paper)
   1. History—Juvenile literature. 2. Reading—Phonetic
  method—Juvenile literature. [1. History. 2. Reading—Phonetic method.]
  I. Title. II. Series.
   D8.B54 2003
   909—dc21   2003006359

Table of Contents

Parent Letter **4**

"Eencey Weencey Spider" . . .**5**

Now and Long Ago **6**

Word List **13**

Word Bingo **14**

Read More **16**

Index **16**

Dear Parent or Caregiver,

Welcome to Compass Point Phonics Readers, books of information for young children. Each book concentrates on specific phonic sounds and words commonly found in beginning reading materials. Featuring eye-catching photographs, every book explores a single science or social studies concept that is sure to grab a child's interest.

So snuggle up with your child, and let's begin. Start by reading aloud the Mother Goose nursery rhyme on the next page. As you read, stress the words in dark type. These are the words that contain the phonic sounds featured in this book. After several readings, pause before the rhyming words, and let your child chime in.

Now let's read *Now and Long Ago*. If your child is a beginning reader, have him or her first read it silently. Then ask your child to read it aloud. For children who are not yet reading, read the book aloud as you run your finger under the words. Ask your child to imitate, or "echo," what he or she has just heard.

Discussing the book's content with your child:
Explain to your child that in most every city or town, you can find buildings or other evidence of how people lived in years past. The photo on page 12 of this book shows a statue of a cowboy in Denver, Colorado, and is a reminder of Colorado's Wild West past. Are there any commemorative statues or monuments in your town that your child can identify?

At the back of the book is a fun Word Bingo game. Your child will take pride in demonstrating his or her mastery of the phonic sounds and the high-frequency words.

Enjoy Compass Point Phonics Readers and watch your child read and learn!

4

Eencey Weencey Spider

Eencey weencey spider
Climbed up the water **spout;**
Down came the rain
And washed poor spider **out.**
Out came the sun
And dried up all the rain;
And the eencey weencey spider
Climbed up the **spout** again.

Life now is not the same as it was long ago. We look at TV. We work and play on computers. We go to schools with many classrooms. Long ago, life was not the same.

This is a school from long ago.
The school had 1 room. Kids of all
ages were in the same class.
They had the same teacher.

This is a farm from long ago.
The farmer used a hand-held plow.
His oxen, horses, or cows pulled
the plow.

Now, farmers use tractors that run on gas. They use machines to plant seeds and harvest crops, too. They can finish their work much faster.

This is a town from long ago.
The streets were made of dirt. People
rode on horses or in coaches. The
houses had no electric lights and no
running water.

Now, streets are paved. Lots of cars and buses go up and down the streets. The houses have electric lights and running water.

Facts about long ago can be found in many places. Find out about your town. Look for things about the past. Ask a grown-up. How has your town changed?

Word List

Diphthong /ou/ *ou*, *ow*

ou
about
found
houses
out

ow
cows
down
how
now
plow
town

High-Frequency
were

Social Studies
computers
electric
room(s)
school(s)
water

Word Bingo

You will need:
- 1 sheet of paper
- 18 game pieces, such as pennies, beans, or checkers

Player 1

cows	about	clouds
found	out	how
town	were	houses

How to Play

- Fold and cut a sheet of paper into 12 pieces. Write each game word on one of the pieces. The words are *about, clouds, cows, down, found, houses, how, now, out, town, were, wow*.
- Fold each piece of paper and put it in a bag or box.
- The players take turns picking a folded paper and reading the word aloud. Each player then covers the word if it appears on his or her game card. The first player to cover 3 words either down, across, or on the diagonal wins. You can also play until the whole card is covered.

Player 2

about	town	out
wow	houses	now
found	down	were

Read More

Isaacs, Sally Senzell. *Life in America's First Cities*. Picture the Past Series. Chicago Ill.: Heinemann Library, 2001.

Roop, Peter, and Connie Roop. *A Home Album*. Long Ago and Today Series. Des Plaines, Ill.: Heinemann Library, 1998.

Scott, Janine. *Life Long Ago*. Minneapolis, Minn.: Compass Point Books, 2003.

Trumbauer, Lisa. *About 100 Years Ago*. Mankato, Minn.: Yellow Umbrella Books, 2000.

Index

buses, 11

cars, 11

computers, 6

crops, 9

electric
  lights, 10, 11

farm, 8

harvest, 9

horses, 8, 10

machines, 9

oxen, 8

plow, 8

school(s), 6,
  7

streets, 10,
  11

teacher, 7

tractors, 9

water, 10,
  11